CHURCH CAN RUIN YOU

AND RELIGION CAN KILL YOU

By
Steve Wolf

ISBN: 978-0-9800907-0-3

For Information Contact
Steve Wolf Ministries
stevewolfministries.wordpress.com
E-mail: s.wolf1@cox.net

Printed in the USA
by Morris Publishing
3212 East Highway 30
Kearney, NE 68847
800-650-7888

Dedication

This book is dedicated to every Christian that has prematurely gone on to be with the Lord, because they never understood their full potential in Christ, due to wrong teaching and false doctrine.

Special Thanks

I offer special thanks to all of my family and friends for all of their love, support, and prayers.

To Dr Tim Tregoning: thank you for boldly following the prompting of the Holy Spirit that day in your office, which helped deliver me from the power of darkness and convey me into the kingdom of the Son of His love.

Table of Contents

Chapter 1

<u>Yoke of Bondage</u>

More people have been killed in the name of religion than anything else. More people have been turned off toward the things of God, because of what they've heard in church, than what they've heard in the world. Jesus said the religious traditions of man make the word of God of no effect. It seems like the majority of churches believe that salvation comes by grace through faith. However, once you've been born again, they spin you around and set a religious yoke of bondage squarely on your shoulders. Gal 5:1 *Stand fast therefore in the liberty by which Christ has made us free, and do not be entangled again with a yoke of bondage.* Even the apostle Paul in his letter to the Galatians, was dumbfounded at their willingness to pick up a religious yoke of bondage. Gal 4:9 *But now after you have known*

God, or rather are known by God, how is it that you turn again to the weak and beggarly elements, to which you desire again to be in bondage? In other words, who, if given a choice, would choose bondage over freedom?

I am not against church, and I know that there are good churches out there, but from what I've experienced they are few and far between. I do not believe we should forsake the assembling of ourselves together. However, I do believe we should be careful who we let speak into our lives. Col 2:9 *Beware lest anyone cheat you through philosophy and empty deceit, according to the basic principles of the world and not according to Christ.*

Chapter 2

<u>Untaught Teachers</u>

I don't believe all the wrong teaching you get in your average church is intentional, as if the pastor were maliciously trying to mislead people. A person can be sincere, but they can be sincerely wrong. Your pastor ought to be hearing from God. 1 Peter 4:11 *If anyone speaks, let him speak as the oracles of God.* We are not to bring our own message to the pulpit. Paul calls us stewards of the mysteries of God, and as stewards, we must be found faithful stewards. We are ambassadors for Christ, we have to deliver the message He's given us. I've heard far too many preachers rant and rave as if they were the voice of God, but don't even have a basic understanding of the difference between the old and new covenants, or how the Kingdom operates. This is why the Bible says that not all should be teachers, for they shall receive a stricter judgment. Heb 13:17 says that those who rule over (or lead) you must give account for your souls. Heb 13:7 *Remember those who rule over you, who have spoken the word of God to you, whose faith follow, considering the outcome of their conduct.* In other words, you can judge a tree by its fruit. Consider the outcome of their conduct. If you are going to play "follow the leader," you'd better be sure the leader is following God.

There is nothing that grieves my heart as much as knowing that entire denominations are misleading the masses about the character and nature of God. They tell people all kinds of nonsense like God will put sickness, diseases, tragedy, poverty, and other forms of death in your life to teach you something, or to serve some form of redemptive purpose. They'll tell people that God is pouring out His wrath on America's sins through hurricanes, earthquakes, 9/11, and other terrorist attacks. They'll say that atonement must be made through varying religious acts before He completely destroys us all. Then they wonder why they can't fill the overflow balcony.

That stuff is absolute garbage! This type of teaching can only come from untaught and unstable people that twist the scripture. When I say untaught, I don't mean ministers that did not attend seminary. I am referring to ministers who weren't taught by the Holy Spirit. 1 Cor 2:13 *These things we also speak, not in words which man's wisdom teaches but which the Holy Spirit teaches.* Even Jesus said that the Holy Spirit would teach us all things, and bring to our remembrance all things He said to us (John 14:26). Eph 4:11 *And He Himself gave some to be apostles, some prophets, some evangelists, and some pastors and teachers.* "And He Himself gave." Let us not put too much importance on framed certificates and diplomas hanging above a desk. Gal 1:1 *Paul, an apostle, not from men nor through man, but through Jesus Christ and God the Father who raised Him from the dead.* Now, I'm not saying that all Bible colleges are bad, or a minister should never go to seminary. However, many of these schools are simply distribution centers for bad doctrine and wrong teaching which will affect millions of people. You can judge for yourself.

Chapter 3

<u>How Arrogant</u>

At the end of the book of Luke, after Jesus had risen from the dead and showed Himself to His disciples; He told them to go and preach the kingdom to all nations beginning in Jerusalem. However, He told them to first tarry in the city of Jerusalem until they were endued with the power from on high. Jesus knew that it would be a natural reaction, after seeing His resurrected body, to want to immediately go out and proclaim it. Acts 1 verse 4 records a sterner tone saying that *He commanded them not to depart from Jerusalem, but to wait for the promise of the Father.* What could be so important, that He would want to keep them from going out and telling the world the greatest news it had ever known? After all, He opened their understanding that they might comprehend the Scriptures (Luke 24:45). Wasn't the knowledge of Jesus' resurrection and comprehension of the Old Testament scriptures enough to go out and preach the Gospel? The answer is no. Acts 1:8 *But you shall receive power when the Holy Spirit has come upon you; and you shall be witnesses to me in Jerusalem, and in all Judea and Samaria, and to the end of the earth.*

It was never God's intention for us to go out in our own power and preach the gospel. However, there are entire mainstream denominations that are doing just that. Jesus commanded His disciples not to go out and preach until they had received the baptism of the Holy Spirit. How arrogant would it be on our part to think that we didn't need to be endued with the power of the Holy Spirit? For the kingdom of God is not in word only, but in demonstration of the Spirit and power. This is not meant to discourage a new believer from sharing his faith. However, we can see by Jesus' example that a person should receive the baptism of the Holy Spirit before filling the office of a preacher. I know that statement draws a line in the sand so to speak, and places well known denominations on the side of error. A prevalent attitude in the body of Christ is to tolerate wrong teaching and often times blasphemous heresies from certain denominations because at least they have the "basics" down.

This is not the attitude Paul had. 1Tim 1:3 *As I urged you when I went to Macedonia- remain in Ephesus that you may charge some that they teach no other doctrine.* 2 Tim 3:16 *All Scripture is given by inspiration of God, and is profitable for doctrine, for reproof, for correction, for instruction...* 2 Tim 4:2 *Preach the word! Be ready in season and out of season. Convince, rebuke, exhort, with all longsuffering and teaching.* Paul did not tolerate false doctrine or wrong teaching, but boldly declared the truth. It does need to be said, that Paul instructed Timothy that *a servant of the Lord must not quarrel but be gentle to all, able to teach, patient, in humility correcting those who are in opposition, if God perhaps will grant them repentance [to change one's thinking] so that they may know the truth* (2 Tim 2:24-25). There is a way to be bold, yet still walk in love.

When Paul went to Ephesus, he was traveling with Aquila and Priscilla. Acts 18: 24-26 *Now a certain Jew named Apollos, born at Alexandria, an eloquent man and mighty in the scriptures, came to Ephesus.*

This man had been instructed in the way of the Lord; and being fervent in spirit, he spoke and taught accurately the things of the Lord, though he knew only the baptism of John. So he began to speak boldly in the synagogue. When Aquila and Priscilla heard him, they took him aside and explained to him the way of the Lord more accurately. This passage of scripture shows us that although Apollos was boldly, and for the most part accurately speaking and teaching the Word of God, Priscilla and Aquila corrected him concerning the baptism of the Holy Spirit. They did not look at each other and say, "Well, at least he's got the basics down."

If a man says that he was called of God to walk in the office of a pastor/preacher, but hasn't received the baptism of the Holy Spirit, was it God that called him? If God truly called him, then Jesus was in error when He told His disciples to wait until they received the baptism. I know there are well known ministers who don't believe in the baptism of the Holy Spirit, but are still bearing fruit. Any time the Word of God goes forth, it will accomplish what it was sent out to accomplish. It can not return void. The Word of God is living and powerful (Heb 4:12). Even so, the scripture teaches us that it is God's plan for New Testament believers to be endued with the power from on high before they minister.

Chapter 4

<u>God Confirms His Word</u>

Talk is cheap. When the paralytic was let down through the roof tiles, Jesus responded to this act of faith and said, "Man, your sins are forgiven you." When the scribes and Pharisees heard this, they were outraged saying only God can forgive sins. Jesus replied, "Which is easier to say, Your sins are forgiven you, or to say, Rise up and walk?" He then told him to rise up and walk. Anyone can walk up to a person and say "Man, your sins are forgiven you." You can't visibly see a sin being forgiven. On the other hand, if you command a paralytic to rise up and walk in the name of Jesus, the results will be verifiable to all.

It is time for the body of Christ as a whole to either put up or shut up. This world has no need for a weak, watered down, powerless gospel. It wasn't good enough for Paul and the rest of the apostles, and it surely won't bring in an end time harvest in our day. Even Jesus didn't begin his earthly ministry until the Holy Spirit descended upon him. When He received the Holy Spirit, that's when He received the miracle working power. He was an example to us in that He was powerful in word and deed. Paul wrote in 1 Cor 2:4 *And my speech and my preaching were not with persuasive words of human wisdom, but in demonstration of the Spirit and of power that your faith should not be in the wisdom of men, but in the power of God.* Acts 4:29b-30 *grant to Your servants that with all boldness they may* **speak Your word, by** *stretching out Your hand to heal, and that signs and wonders may be done through the name of Your holy child Jesus.* Notice that the disciples asked God to speak His word through them by the performing of miracles. They were saying that the working of miracles is part of preaching the Word. Those who separate speaking the Word from doing the Word are not following the New Testament example.

If a Christian and a Muslim were to have a debate with the goal of converting the other person, relying on doctrine alone would most likely reach a dead end. Each has their own set of beliefs, could back them up with their scripture, and believes they are right. However, if the Christian took the attitude of Elijah, there would be no need for further debate. 1 Kings 18:21 *and Elijah came to all the people, and said, "How long will you waiver between two opinions? If the Lord is God, follow Him; but, if Baal, follow him."* He went on to say that he alone would go against the 450 prophets of Baal. He said that they would each build an altar. 1 Kings 18:24 *Then you call on the name of your gods, and I will call on the name of the Lord; and the God who answers by fire, He is God.* In other words, it's time to put up or shut up. Needless to say their god did not send fire down; but there was no voice, no one answered, no one paid attention (1 Kings 18:29). Even after Elijah soaked his offering with water three times, *the fire of the Lord fell and consumed the burnt sacrifice, and the wood and the stones and the dust, and licked up the water that was in the trench* (1 Kings 18:38). Now let's suppose the Christian preached the gospel to the Muslim, operated in the gifts of the Spirit by receiving a word of knowledge, laid hands on the man, and saw an instantaneous healing of the disease he had for 3 years. The debate would most likely be over. Even Jesus said, "If you don't believe Me, at least believe for the sake of the works that I do."

When Elijah issued the challenge to the prophets of Baal, the people agreed and said it was well spoken. I believe people today would love to see a challenge of the same sorts. However, most preachers would rather just talk about the miracle working power of God then actually demonstrate it. I recently heard a preacher boldly proclaim the Word of God concerning healing for a full forty minutes. After he was done, he had an altar call for anyone that needed healing. After fifteen or twenty people came forward, a blind man tapping his walking stick gradually made his way to the altar. You could visibly see the fear and unbelief on the preacher's face. Needless to say he never even prayed for the blind man. In fact, I don't believe there were any manifestations at the altar that day. The Bible says that God confirms the preaching of His Word with signs and wonders following. God is always willing to perform His Word, but we have to step out there in faith with no doubting to see it come to pass.

Chapter 5

<u>Brood of Vipers!</u>

When Jesus walked on the Earth, He gave us a perfect example of how to walk in love toward our fellow man. After all, He is the Prince of Peace. Matt 23:27 *Woe to you scribes and Pharisees, hypocrites! For you are like whitewashed tombs which indeed appear beautiful outwardly, but inside are full of dead men's bones and all uncleanness*. Matt 23:37 *Serpents, brood of vipers! How can you escape the condemnation of hell?* Wow, it sounds like Jesus had a righteous anger against the religious teachings of the scribes and Pharisees. In the book of Matthew alone, He called them: fools, blind guides, hypocrites, wicked, evil, faithless, perverse, adulterous, and sons of the devil to name a few. Why is it that Jesus reacted so strongly against them? Why did He rebuke them so sharply?

Matt 23:4 *For they bind heavy burdens, hard to bear, and lay them on men's shoulders; but they themselves will not move them with one of their fingers.* He hated the way their religious traditions and doctrines of man kept the people under a yoke that was hard to bear. He also hated the way their traditions kept the people's hearts far from God; focusing on outward acts of holiness. These acts and regulations put down so many requirements for salvation that people despaired of ever being good enough to be accepted by God. This is also typical for the modern day Pharisees we have in the church today.

Remember this; religion will always have you focus on your outward acts of holiness, neglecting the condition of your heart. Religious people will teach that right standing or righteousness with God is accomplished through holy actions, and keeping various commandments. Matt 23:13 *But woe to you, scribes and Pharisees, hypocrites! For you shut up the kingdom of heaven against men; for you neither go in yourselves, nor do you allow those who are entering to go in.* This is one of the main reasons I am writing this book. Once again, religious traditions and doctrines of man make the

Word of God of no effect. There are droves of people out there that have been saved, but then were poisoned by religious teaching to the point where Christ is profiting them nothing in this life. Gal 3:3 *Are you so foolish? Having begun in the Spirit, are you now being made perfect by the flesh?* Jesus is the author and finisher of our faith. It is time for the body of Christ to look again to our author. It is time for us to exalt the Word of God to its rightful position of complete and total authority in our lives. We need to place it far above anything that comes out of the pulpit, or was handed down from our parents or grandparents. Personally I am appalled at the amount of religious teaching that has been so widely accepted, so blindly swallowed by the masses of Christians for generations. Enough is enough! It ends here! It is time to shake off the chains and be the church that God has called us to be. Christian- sharpen your axe, grab your sword, gird up your loins, its cow killing time!

Chapter 6

Killing Cows

The term religious cow usually refers to a sacredly held belief that has some how been passed down from generation to generation. This next chapter may sting a little. You may want to get offended by the truths I am about to share. Some of these truths may be contrary to everything you've ever been taught in church. Let me ask you this. How is your current belief system working out for you? Are you living the abundant life that Jesus came and died on the cross to give us? Are you full of joy and peace? Are you prospering in every area of your life? Does your church resemble the New Testament church of Paul's day with the power of God regularly being manifested? If not, perhaps we should reexamine our doctrine and root out any religion of man that might have crept in making the Word of God of no effect.

Romans 3:4 says *let God be true but every man a liar.* Don't be so quick to dismiss the things in this chapter simply because your brain tells you they can't be true. I believe if you listen to the still small voice of the Holy Spirit, He will bear witness to these truths and lead and guide you into all truth.

I suppose if a person were to try to counter all the wrong religious teaching out there, they would deplete a small forest in paper alone. There's a lot of weirdness out there. It's amazing how far we can stray from the truth in a little over 2,000 years. I'm only going to kill what I believe to be the most common and therefore most damaging sacred cows. I have divided this chapter into 4 sections. Now remember, I am not trying to condemn anyone. My aim is to use the scripture for doctrine, reproof, correction, and instruction (2 Tim 3:16).

Extreme Sovereignty of God

Let's call the first cow "Extreme Sovereignty of God" doctrine. This is the belief that God is sovereignly in control of absolutely everything in the world, and that nothing happens without His consent or approval. Extreme versions say that everything has been predetermined or preordained, and no matter what we do, God's plan in our life is going to come to pass. This gives the impression that you are just a little rubber ducky floating around in the great ocean of life being tossed to and fro with no power to do anything. You'll hear things like "Well you know, brother, we're just clay in the potter's hands." I don't mind being called a lump of clay, but know this; this lump was predestined to be conformed to the image of His Son – that same Son that He declared, "This is my beloved Son in whom I am well pleased."

I do believe that God is sovereign in that He is first in rank and order. He answers to no one and is above all. No Christian would dispute that. The biggest problem with this extreme sovereignty of God doctrine is that it makes God responsible for every evil thing that happens on this earth. As I mentioned in Chapter 1 every tragedy whether it's an illness, a hurricane, or a severe birth defect, all gets blamed on God. They'll say, "Well brother if God puts cancer on you, breaks up your marriage, kills your baby, and allows your dog to get run over, it's because He's trying to teach you something or work some sort of redemption purpose in your life." I don't know about you, but I wouldn't want to surrender my life to a God like that. The devil loves hearing preaching like that. This doctrine will turn people away from God by the droves.

Ask someone to defend this position and they'll say, "The Lord works in mysterious ways," or "You never know what the Lord's going to do". Oh really, what about Eph 5:17? *Therefore do not be unwise, but understand what the will of the Lord is.* Jesus said if you've seen me, you've seen the Father. The mystery has been revealed! Eph 1:9 *having made known to us the mystery of His will, according to His good pleasure which He purposed in Himself.* Col 1:26 *the mystery which has been hidden from the ages and from generations, but* now has been revealed to His saints. *John 15:15 No longer do I call you servants, for a servant does not know what his master is doing, but I have called you friends, for all things that I heard from My Father I have made known to you.* If you are a Christian, you should not be ignorant of God's will. If you are, you need to crack open your Bible because His Word is His will.

You wouldn't even have to read very far before you started to disprove this sovereignty of God doctrine. *Gen 1:27-28 So God created man in His own image; in the image of God He created Him; male and female He created them. Then God blessed them, and God said to them, "Be fruitful and multiply fill the earth and subdue it; have dominion over the fish of the sea, over the birds of the air, and over every living thing that moves on the earth."* God gave mankind power and dominion over the earth. Adam and Eve yielded that power over to Satan. However, Jesus came to seek and to save that which was lost. He gave us back the original power and dominion that God intended for us to have from the beginning.

Most people assume that since God is God, he could do absolutely anything on this earth. I would agree that He has that ability; however, He chose to exalt His Word above all else. God is not a man that He should lie. God has basically tied His own hands so to speak when He gave us dominion over the earth. In other words, He's not going to do something that He told us to do. For example, a person will beg and plead with God to save a relative of theirs even though the Bible clearly instructs **us** to go into all the world and preach the gospel. Or they'll say God I need some money, and I know you can do anything, so please give me some money. Even though the Bible says that He gives **us** the power to get wealth, and as we give, it will be given back to us.

Perhaps the biggest false assumption is that whatever God wills to take place on the earth, has to happen. A person will pray to God to heal them, and if it doesn't seem to work, they'll just assume it must not have been God's will for them to be healed. After all, God is God and if He really wanted them to be healed, they'd be healed, right? 2 Peter 3:9 says that *God is not willing that any should perish, but that all should come to repentance.* It is not God's will that anyone should go to hell. However, Jesus said that there would be more people entering the broad gate to hell than the narrow gate to heaven. These scriptures clearly show us that God's will doesn't automatically come to pass. The same is true for the healing of our bodies.

When Jesus walked on this earth, He was literally the physical manifestation of God's will (John 1:1, 14). He said He could only do what He saw the Father do, and say what the Father told Him to say. Matt 9:35 *Then Jesus went about all the cities and villages, teaching in the synagogues, and preaching the gospel of the kingdom, and healing* **every** *sickness and* **every** *disease among the people.* In fact, there was not one account of Jesus turning down someone for healing that came to Him to be healed. Acts 10:38 *how God anointed Jesus of Nazareth with the Holy Spirit and with power, who went about doing good and healing* **all** *who were oppressed by the devil, for God was with Him.* Since Jesus Christ is the same yesterday, today, and forever, we can see it is still God's will for all to be healed.

Instead of asking God to do things for us that He told us to do, we need to start operating in the power and authority that we've been given. In Matt 28:18, Jesus said, *"all authority has been given to Me in* heaven and on earth. *Go therefore and make disciples out of all nations…"* The power has been transferred. In John 17:18, Jesus was praying to God for His disciples and said, *"as you have sent Me into the world, I also have sent them into the world".* He goes on to say in verse 20, *"I do not pray for these alone, but also for those who will believe in me through their word."* He is talking about us! Therefore as God sent Jesus into the world; mighty in word and deed, Jesus sends us into the world in like manner. This, of course, is after we've been endued with the power from on high. John 14:12 *Most assuredly, I say to you, he that believes in Me, the works that I do he will do also, and greater works than these he will do because I go to My Father.* Most Christians readily accept the first half of Ephesians 3:20; *Now to Him who is able to do exceedingly abundantly above all that we ask or think,* but struggle with the last half; *according to the power that works in us.* I believe this is because the church as a whole has been beating people down telling them how much of a worm they are, and how unworthy they are. I will be addressing this issue a little later.

Finally, it's not God that allows bad things to happen. It's actually us, or the fact that we live in a fallen world. As I said before, we are the ones that have been given authority on this earth. James 4:7 says *submit to God, resist the devil, and he will flee from you.* The word "resist" means to actively fight against. You can't actively fight against something like sickness or poverty if you don't know whether or not it's from God. John 10:10 says that *the thief comes only to steal, kill, and destroy.* If you are still unsure, go back to Deuteronomy chapter 28. God says that sickness and poverty are curses-- not blessings from God. Galatians 3:13 says that Christ has redeemed us from the curse of the law so that the blessings may come upon us through faith in Him. Being ignorant of God's Word and swallowing anything that is preached to you can get you into serious trouble, and even kill you. God says my people perish from lack of knowledge. The devil preys on ignorance of the Word in that he walks about as a roaring loin seeking whom he may devour. That is why it is so important this sovereignty of God doctrine is exposed. Far too many Christians are dying young because they're sitting with their hands in their pockets waiting to see if God, perhaps, might maybe want them healed- if it be His will. Oh Christian, take your hands out of your pockets, lay them on the sick and watch them recover like the Bible instructs us! Don't you understand that when the devil attacks us with symptoms in our bodies, or anything else contrary to God's Word, he is bluffing? He's just waiting to see if anyone is going to use their God given authority to call his bluff and command him to leave in the name of Jesus.

I once ministered to a group of kids that suffered severe burns and other physical defects. I explained to them that it wasn't God who caused these tragedies to happen in their lives. I told them that only the thief comes to steal, kill, and destroy. Finally, I explained the true character and nature of God. The kids received the message with open arms, but I could see that some of the adults didn't agree with the message. It is a convenient doctrine to think that God is in complete control of everything, and nothing happens without His stamp of approval. People take comfort in that because it takes any and all responsibility off of them. This man made religious sovereignty of God doctrine has been ruining people's lives for long enough.

God is Angry!

God is angry! He sees all of our sins, and is pouring out His wrath on us! Although your pastor may have preached that last Sunday, it is simply not true. Let's call this second widely accepted, deeply embedded religious cow "God is angry!" There are many religious leaders that think the only difference between the Old Testament and the New Testament is that blank page between Malachi and Matthew. They're still singing all the Psalms and preaching all the Proverbs even though a large number of them do not apply to a born again New Testament believer. God is not dealing with us the same way He dealt with people under the old covenant. We have a new and better covenant which Isaiah spoke of in chapter 54 verse 9. *For this is* [the new covenant] *like the waters of Noah to me; For as I have sworn that the waters of Noah would no longer cover the earth, so have I sworn that I would not be angry with you, nor rebuke you.* God is saying that this new covenant is like the one He made with Noah when

He promised He would never flood the earth again. It was unconditional, and was not contingent on the people. He did not say that He would not flood the earth again as long as they did not turn there backs on Him again. Isaiah goes on to say in verse 10 *For the mountains shall depart and the hills be removed, but my kindness shall not depart from you, Nor shall My **covenant of peace** be removed.* Sadly enough, there are a lot of people that haven't even heard that there was a covenant of peace. Although they bare some responsibility, their ignorance is not entirely their fault since this is not the message the majority of churches are preaching. After all, *faith comes by hearing and hearing by the word of God.* (Rom 10:17)

I am now going to use one of my favorite passages of scripture to expand on the Gospel of Peace. 2 Cor 5:18-19 *Now all things are of God, who has reconciled us to Himself through Jesus Christ, and has given us the ministry of reconciliation, that is, that God was in Christ reconciling the world to Himself, not imputing their trespasses to them, and has committed to us the word of reconciliation.* These scriptures tell us that God is no longer imputing our sins unto us. The word impute is an accounting term that means to lay to the account of. Each time you sin, the charge is not going to your account, it's going to Jesus' account and He's already paid the bill!

Let me further explain. The first two thousand years of man's existence God was not imputing man's sins against him. *Sin was in the world, but sin is not imputed when there is no law* (Rom 5:13). Once the law was given through Moses sin **was** imputed to man. God showed mercy to Cain the first murderer, but killed a man for breaking the law by picking up sticks on the Sabbath. The law was in force for two thousand years and during that time, the wrath of God was being poured out against sin, due to the impossible to keep requirements of the law. When Jesus finally came, He ushered in the age of the dispensation of grace. People have been living in this age of grace for roughly two thousand years. Sadly, most people are completely oblivious to this truth and still believe God is holding their sins against them.

Colossians 2:13-14 *And you, being dead in your trespasses and the uncircumcision of your flesh, He has made alive together with Him, having forgiven you all trespasses, having wiped out the handwriting of requirements that was against us which was contrary to us. And He has taken it out of the way, having nailed it to the cross.* Wow, that says a lot. Those two verses seem so straightforward to me that I'm not even going to comment on them accept to say, "Praise God!"

I feel I have been holding back, so now I'm going to be blunt. To a certain degree, sin is not even an issue with God anymore. It's not. He's not even concerned about it. Do you know why? His wrath toward sin has been appeased, there's been an atonement. The price for all sin, for all mankind has been paid. David knew that this age of grace was coming when he said *"Blessed are those whose lawless deeds are forgiven, and whose sins are covered; Blessed is the man to whom the Lord **shall not** impute sin."* David understood that there was coming a time where there would be peace from God towards man. John the Baptist's father also prophesied of what Jesus would do saying that we *"Might serve Him* [God] **without fear,** *in holiness and righteousness before Him all the days of our life"* (Luke 1:74-75). Finally, the angels understood this saying *"Glory to God in the highest, and on earth peace,* *goodwill* [from God] *towards men!"* (Luke 2:14).

Jesus did it. He did what all the animal sacrifices and burnt offerings under the old covenant could not do. When Jesus was lifted up on the cross, He drew all of God's judgment and wrath for our sins upon Himself like a big lightening rod. Jesus in His own words said, "It is finished!" For the most part the modern day church has echoed "no its not" in response. Rom 10:3 *For they being ignorant of God's righteousness, and seeking to establish their own righteousness, have not submitted to the righteousness of God.* This verse is saying that people like to make up their own beliefs on how to be in right standing with God. It just makes sense to our human brains that we should have to do good or holy acts to earn favor or right standing with God. This might be why every religion has its own set of rules, codes, or creeds that earn you right standing with their god.

Christianity, or should I say true Christianity is the only religion where righteousness is obtained by grace (apart from any goodness, works, or merit on our part) through faith in a savior. 2 Cor 5:21 *For He made Him who knew no sin to be sin for us, that we might become the righteousness of God in Him.* Romans chapter three and four both explain faith righteousness. I would advise reading both chapters, but for now I'll summarize. *Therefore by the deeds of the law no flesh will be justified in His sight* (Rom 3:20). *But now the righteousness of God apart from the law is revealed* (Rom 3:21). *Therefore we conclude that a man is justified by faith apart from the deeds of the law* (Rom 3:28). Rom 5:1 *Therefore having been justified by faith,* **we have peace with God** *through our Lord Jesus Christ.* Rom 5:9 *Much more then, having now been justified by His blood, we shall be* **saved from wrath** *through Him.* I honestly believe the message of our faith-based righteousness is so prevalent throughout the New Testament, that you would have to have a self-righteous or religious type person to help you misunderstand it.

I made the statement earlier that sin wasn't really an issue with God anymore. Now, before you take this book outside and burn it, let me explain. God is a spirit, and those who worship Him **must** worship Him in spirit and truth (John 4:24). This is important, because in order to understand my statement, you have to see yourself the way God sees you. Religion looks at you in your flesh, but since God is a spirit, He looks at you in your born-again spirit. 2 Cor 5:17 *Therefore if anyone is in Christ, he is a new creation; old things have passed away; behold, all things have become new.* Before a person gets saved, they have the spirit of the world, not the spirit of God dwelling in them. Eph 2:3 says that they *were by nature children of wrath.* This is due to the fall of Adam. Rom 5:18 *Therefore, as through one man's offense judgment came to all men, resulting in condemnation.* Before we were saved, we did in fact have a sin nature.

You are made up of three parts; you are a spirit, you have a soul (your mind, thoughts, and emotions), and you live in a body. When the scripture says you are a new creation, old things have passed away, all things have become new; it's talking about your spirit. It is not talking about your soul or your body. In other words if you have grey hair and are bad at math before you get saved, you're still going to have grey hair and poor math skills after salvation. However, your old spirit, or sin nature, or as the Bible often calls it, "old man" was crucified with Christ. It's dead and gone. According to Romans 8:9 we receive the Spirit of Christ at salvation, we are therefore a new creation. This is what it means to be born-again. Verse 11 goes on to say that the spirit of Him who raised Jesus from the dead dwells in us. Our new born-again spirit was created in righteousness and true holiness (Eph 4:24). When God looks at us now, we are holy, blameless, and above reproach in His sight. (Col 1:22) In your born again spirit, you are as clean and holy and pure as Jesus is. As He is in heaven, so are we in this world (1 John 4:17). Some of you might have a hard time believing that you actually have the spirit of Christ on the inside of you. Rom 8:9 *Now if anyone does not have the Spirit of Christ he is not His.* That pretty much settles it, doesn't it? This is how Paul could say it is no longer I who live, but Christ who lives in me. The moment you get born again God gives you a new spirit, the Spirit of His Son, which was created in righteousness and true holiness, and is in fact perfect. It is then sealed for the day of redemption (Eph 4:30). Eph 1:13-14 also says we were sealed with the Holy Spirit of promise until the redemption of the purchased possession (our bodies). Sin can not penetrate your born-again spirit since it was made perfect, and then sealed. Understanding and receiving this truth is the only way to interpret 1 John 3:9, *Whoever has been born of God does not sin, for His seed remains in him; and he cannot sin, because he has been born of God.* This verse confirms two things. First, we know that Christians do sin. We can both observe this, and prove this in scripture (1 John 2:1). To say *"whosever has been born of God does not sin,"* you would have to be looking at us the way God does through our born-again spirits. Secondly, *"for His seed remains in him"* shows that the seed (which is the spirit of Christ in us) can not be corrupted or penetrated by sin. So what am I saying? Am I saying that since your spirit has been perfected forever, and God is no longer imputing our sins unto us, we might as well go live in sin? Absolutely not!

Sin affects us in two ways: vertically (up and down) and laterally (side to side). Vertically, God is not holding our sins against us because He laid them on Jesus. However, He is concerned about the affects sin has in our lives and other people's. Sin will not change God's love toward us, but it will change our love towards God. Sin hardens our hearts toward the things of God. The lateral effects of sin are destroying people's lives here on earth. When you sin, you give Satan an open door to your soul (your mind, thoughts, emotions) as well as an opportunity to destroy your physical body. Gal 6:8 *He that sows unto the flesh will of the flesh reap corruption.* Not only that, but you will be affecting other people's lives in a negative way.

The apostle Paul gave us several reasons for not living in sin. Rom 6:16 *Do you not know that to whom you present yourselves slaves to obey, you are that one's slave whom you obey, whether of sin leading to death, or of obedience leading to righteousness?* Jesus came to set us free from sin. Rom 6:14 *For sin shall not have dominion over you, for you are not under law but under grace.* Sin no longer has dominion over us, but we can choose to yield to it, cutting short our lives here on earth by allowing some form of death to creep into our bodies, or soulish realm. Paul asks this question in Rom 6:2 *"How shall we who died to sin live any longer in it?"* He goes on to say, *"knowing that our old man was crucified with Him".* Contrary to popular teaching, we no longer have a sin nature. You'll hear people say, "Well brother Joe fell into sin, he must have been tempted beyond what he could bear. After all we're only human; just a bunch of sinners saved by grace." No! We are a new creation. Old things have passed away. Christians do not have a sin nature. You have to renew your mind to this truth. An unrenewed mind will make you feel like sin is still in your nature. The truth is, all of the fruits of the Spirit are alive and well in our new born- again spirit.

Before I can completely kill the sacred "God is angry" cow, I must address one last subject. Not only has God forgiven Christians of their sins, but He has also forgiven the sins of lost people. 1 John 2:1 *And He (Jesus) Himself is the propitiation for our sins, and not for ours only but also for the whole world.* The word propitiation is defined as: To appease the wrath of God so that His justice and holiness will be satisfied and He can forgive sin. Titus 2:4 *For the grace of God that brings salvation has appeared to all men.* Even though the payment for sin was made, and God has forgiven everyone's sins, people still have to receive the payment for their sins by accepting Jesus as their Lord and Savior.

You might want to brace yourself for this next truth because it is so contrary to what we've been taught. People do not go to hell for the individual sins they commit. We'll tell people that if they've broken any of the Ten Commandments, that's what will send them to hell.

People go to hell for one reason; they reject the payment for their sins which is Jesus Christ. Mark 3:28-29 *Assuredly, I say to you, all sins will be forgiven the sons of men, and whatever blasphemies they may utter: "but he who blasphemes against the Holy Spirit never has forgiveness, but is subject to eternal condemnation."* Here's another truth that goes along with that. You can not lose your salvation like you lose your car keys. You can not sin it away, since sin does not penetrate your born again spirit that has been perfected forever and sealed for redemption. You can; however, reject your salvation. Sin plays a huge role in this. Continually walking in sin will harden your heart toward the things of God. The scripture teaches that you could become so hardened that you can actually consciously renounce your faith in Jesus. Paul explains in Hebrews 6:4-6 that there are still qualifications that must be met before a person can reject their salvation. He teaches that a person must have heard the gospel, received salvation, received the baptism of the Holy Spirit, seen the Word of God work in their life, and operated in the gifts of the Spirit. In other words, they have to be a relatively mature Christian. It is then and only then that God will give them over to a debased mind.

I believe I need to add one more thing before we move on. There is coming a time when God will judge the earth. Most Bible scholars would agree that it is soon or very soon. People who have rejected Jesus will have to face the righteous judgment of God. However, we are instructed to *judge nothing before the time* (1 Cor 4:5). John 12:48 *"He who rejects Me, and does not receive My words, has that which judges him – the word that I have spoken will judge him in the last day."* For the time being, we are living in the age of the dispensation of God's grace. Let us all thank Jesus for that! 2 Cor 5:18 *Now all things are of God, who has reconciled us to Himself through Jesus Christ, and has given us the ministry of reconciliation.* 2 Cor 5:20 *Now then, we are ambassadors for Christ, as though God were pleading through us, we implore you on Christ's behalf, be reconciled to God.* Fellow Christian, let us go against the religious tide, and let us take this message to the world: God loves you, His wrath has been appeased, He's not angry!

1 John 1:9 and Sin Consciousness

Now it's time to kill the largest, shiniest, most sacred, beloved, and greatly worshipped religious cow of all. This cow crosses all denominational lines, and has been placed on a pedestal that rises higher than the tower of Babel. Most Christians polish this cow daily, if not several times a day. That being said, it's still hard to place a name on it, so I'm calling it the "1 John 1:9 cow" and to a lesser extent "sin consciousness."

When some Christians pray, the first thing they do is ask God to forgive them of all the sins they may have committed that day. Some believe that they can actually lose their salvation if they don't get every sin confessed and "under the blood". Or at the very least, they feel that God won't bless them or hear their prayers if their sins are in the way. This type of thinking causes a person to become sin conscious which means they truly don't understand the grace of their salvation through Jesus. This thinking for the most part is brought on by a misinterpretation of 1 John 1:9: *If we confess our sins,*

He is faithful and just to forgive us our sins and to cleanse us from all unrighteousness.

It is not good Bible interpretation to take one scripture and make a doctrine out of it. The Bible says by the mouth of two or three witnesses every word shall be established. We cannot accept a truth in God's word if it violates other truths in God's word. Let me submit to you three possible ways of interpreting 1 John 1:9. I will start with the way I believe we should interpret this verse. If you have received the truths in this book up to this point, this should be easily understood. First, let's look at this verse in context. Verse 7 says that *the blood of Jesus Christ His Son cleanses us from **all** sin.* Verse 8 says *If we say that we have **no sin**, we deceive ourselves, and the truth is not in us.* I believe this must be talking about the initial salvation experience. The word "sin," not "sins" is used which implies sin nature. If we say that we have no sin nature, we deceive ourselves. Another reason I believe it's talking about the initial salvation experience, is because verse 9 ends with *"cleanse us from all unrighteousness."* Why would a Christian need to be cleansed from unrighteousness when we've been made the righteousness of God through Christ? After all 1 John 3:9 says *"Whosever has been born of God does not sin."* Verse 10 really makes my point for me, *"If we say that we have not sinned* (past tense*), we make Him a liar, and His word is not in us.* We would make Him a liar because His word says that all have sinned and fallen short of the glory of God. No Christian would ever say that they have not sinned. Only a self-righteous person who hasn't submitted to God's faith-based righteousness would say that. A Christian by definition has to believe in righteousness by faith. *For with the heart one believes unto righteousness and with the mouth confession is made unto salvation* (Roman 10:10). One definition of the word "confess" means to plead guilty. When you admit that you are guilty of sin and receive the payment for sin by putting your faith in Jesus Christ, God is faithful and just to forgive you and to cleanse you from all unrighteousness. I conclude that 1 John 1:7 says that when you are a Christian, the blood of Jesus Christ cleansed us from all sin. Verses 8, 9, and 10 are speaking to a person who will not admit they are guilty of sin. Verse 9 gives the remedy.

I have heard another possible interpretation that lines up with the Word, and what I've been teaching.

Once again, we are made up of three parts spirit, soul, and body (1 Thes 5:23). When you confess your sins, God brings that forgiveness that's already a reality in your spirit realm into your soulish realm and body. This goes right along with James 5:15 *and the prayer of faith will save the sick, and the Lord will raise him up. And if he has committed sins, he will be forgiven.* These three scriptures James 5:14-16 are all speaking about being healed from sickness in your body. Your spirit was sealed at salvation, but sin can open the door for the enemy to bring his form of death (sickness, depression) into your soulish realm or body. When we repent (change our thinking or direction) we slam the door shut; therefore, we no longer give place to the devil, and are bodies are healed.

Finally, we come to the third interpretation which the church as a whole has embraced, despite the fact that it goes against a multitude of scripture and biblical principals. As I mentioned earlier, we can't accept a passage of scripture as a truth if it violates other truths in God's Word. There are no mistakes in the Bible; *His ways are perfect and His word is proven* (Ps 18:30). All scriptures, no matter how contrary they first appear to be, will harmonize with correct interpretation. When you take 1 John 1:9 out of context and at face value, you can come up with a doctrine that the forgiveness of our sins is based on our confession of each individual sin. You could then say that any sin that you don't confess and, "get under the blood," can't be forgiven. Our forgiveness, and ultimately our salvation would be placed on our shoulders. It would also hinge on our ability to even recognize every sin we've committed. That's quite an impossible load for someone to bear. Maybe that's why God sent Jesus to bear it for us.

I have good news for you. God has forgiven all of your sins; past, present, and even the sins you will commit in the future. Can God forgive a sin before you commit it? You'd better believe it since Jesus only died for our sins once over two thousand years ago. The prevalent thought in the body of Christ is that when you get born again, all of the past sins you have committed up to that point are forgiven. After that, each sin you commit is a new affront against God, and it is your responsibility to recognize it, confess it, and ask for forgiveness. Gal 3:3 *Are you so foolish? Having begun in the Spirit, are you now being made perfect by the flesh?* Anyone that ascribes to this thinking is basically saying "Yes, Jesus paid a price, but it wasn't a full price; we still have to add our confession and petition for forgiveness each time we sin." To me it sounds like Christians are still trying to bring an offering for their sins through their actions. Heb 7:27 *who does not need daily, as those high priest, to offer up sacrifices, first for His own sins and then for the people's, for this He did **once for all** when He offered up Himself.* We need to quit trying to be our own savior, and put faith in the Savior and believe Him when He declared "It is finished!"

The most damaging aspect of adopting a doctrine based on a wrong interpretation of 1 John 1:9 is that it causes a person to become sin conscious. Such a person is living their life in bondage. I believe that the following teaching, if received, will set people free.

The origin of sin consciousness can be traced back to the Garden of Eden. When Adam ate the fruit, man became sin conscious. It was never God's original plan for us to be that way. His plan was for us to have close fellowship with Him, letting Him teach us the ways that we should walk on the earth. We can see that this is true because after Adam fell, sin was in the world, but without the law, sin was not imputed. It wasn't until Moses that God gave the law. The law was only temporary, a tutor, a type and shadow of things to come. In order to cleanse or purge their conscious from sin, the people would have to come to the priest who would daily offer up sacrifices for his own sins, and then for their sins. These priests would also have to make a sacrifice and offering once a year for all the peoples' sins committed out of ignorance (Heb 9:7). Heb 9:9 *It was symbolic for the present time in which both gifts and sacrifices are offered which cannot make him who performed the services perfect **in regard to conscience**.* This is saying that the Old Testament system of sacrifices could never completely cleanse the conscience from sin. People remained sin conscious. However, our high priest (Jesus) established a new covenant with us making the old one obsolete. Heb 9:12-14 *Not with the blood of goats and calves, but with His own blood He entered the Most Holy Place once for all, having obtained **eternal redemption**. For if the blood of bulls and goats and the ashes of a heifer, sprinkling the unclean, sanctifies for the purifying of the flesh, how much more shall the blood of Christ, who* through the eternal Spirit offered Himself without spot to God, **cleanse your conscience from dead works** to serve the living God? Jesus was the perfect spotless sinless sacrifice that God was looking for. His sacrifice is the only thing that can purge our conscience from sin consciousness; and for what purpose? - to serve the living God.

Hebrews 10:1-2 basically says that if the Old Testament sacrifices could have made the people perfect would they not have ceased to be offered? For the worshippers, once purified, would have had **no more consciousness of sins**. This is it! This is my whole point. God sent His Son, the perfect sacrifice so that you would have no more consciousness of sins! Simply put, if you walk around all day with a mental notebook that you use to record every sin you commit that day so that you later can confess it, or "get it under the blood," you will be of little use for the things of God. This type of behavior will cause you to be self-centered, and sin conscious instead of God conscious. Heb 10:23 let us draw near with a true heart in full assurance of faith, having our hearts sprinkled from an **evil conscience**. We have to assure our hearts before Him

(1 John 3:19). 1 John 3:20 *For if our heart* [conscience] *condemns us, God is greater than our hearts and knows all things.* I've heard it said "sin makes cowards of men," because it makes you feel guilty, your conscience condemns you, and you don't feel worthy and have no confidence towards God. 1 John 3:21 *Beloved if our heart does not condemn us, we have confidence toward God.*

Some people think that their conscience is always right, or is probably the Holy Spirit talking to them. The truth is, only Satan is the accuser of the brethren. Your conscience can condemn you even when you have done nothing wrong. This is especially true with self imposed religious traditions of men. John 3:*17 For God did not send His Son to condemn the world –* but there are plenty of preachers who feel that this is what they're here for. Remember this; religion always tries to take the simplicity out of the Gospel. Religion always tries to make you focus on your external actions and trying to make you holy by keeping a list of requirements or commandments that often vary by denomination. When I was a teenager, I attended a church that thought that if you danced, you were of the devil. I guess they never read how David danced before the Lord until his clothes fell off. Most of the seniors didn't dance at their prom. The ones that did dance were up at the altar on Sunday begging for forgiveness, thinking that God was condemning them. The truth is, their own conscience was condemning them, because they had been sitting under wrong teaching.

It was never God's original plan for mankind to be sin conscious. This is one of the reasons He told Adam not to eat of the tree of the knowledge of good and evil. He knew that the first thing that would happen was that we would become self conscious. Adam and Eve confirmed this when they immediately covered themselves. He wanted us to be God conscious. Man fully became sin conscious after God gave the law. However, He had to because mankind was heading toward a state of decline that would have made God's plan of redemption impossible. So the law made us sin conscious, but God sent Jesus to purge our conscious from dead works to serve the living God. He has also *made us alive together with Him, having wiped out the handwriting of requirements, that was against us that was contrary to us. And He has taken it out of the way, having nailed it to the cross.* (Col 2:13-14)

We are New Testament saints. We are under a new and better covenant. When we miss the mark, we don't have to fall on our faces before God and cry a puddle of tears and beg for forgiveness. We are instructed to come boldly to the throne of grace. When you beg God to forgive your sins here's what you're really saying. "Father God, despite what your Word says, I don't believe that the atonement of Jesus was enough. I don't think that I'm righteous, justified, blameless, and above reproach in your eyes like your Word says. I don't believe there was enough power in the blood of Jesus to cleanse all of my sins, but just enough to cleanse the one that I committed before salvation. I don't believe that my born- again spirit was created in righteousness and true holiness, and is in fact the Spirit of Christ living in me. Therefore, I ask you to forgive me of all my sins – again. Oh wait, first I have to confess each individual one. This could take a while. I hope you're not too busy God… and on and on and on… in Jesus' name. Amen." All God really wants us to do is repent and go on! To repent is to turn from, head the opposite direction, or to change one's thinking. One of the reason's Christianity is not having more of an affect on our society is most Christian don't know who they are in Christ and are still sin conscious. Phil 1:6 *that the sharing of your faith may become effective by the acknowledgement of every good thing which is in you in Christ Jesus.*

Obedience and the Blessing

I feel compelled to slaughter one last religious cow before continuing on with the book. This sacred cow has been around for a while, but has recently become quite popular and prevalent. Let's call this cow "obedience and the blessing." The simplest way of describing this doctrine is to say that God's blessings are based on our performance. You'll hear things like "you can't expect God to bless you if you have any sin in your life." Here's an oldie but goodie, "God can't use a dirty vessel." The slogan that today's church has adopted is "sin blocks the blessing." I could see why this line of thinking would make sense to the natural mind.

Everything in our society is performance based. You could even say that this performance based system is a basic principal of the world. Col 2:8 *Beware lest anyone cheat you through philosophy and empty deceit, according to the tradition of men, according to the basic principals of the world and not according to Christ.* This scripture is a warning that for the most part has been ignored by the body of Christ. Grace is the exact opposite of the world's performance based system.

Romans 1:16 *"For I am not ashamed of the gospel of Christ, for it is the power of God to salvation for everyone who believes..."* This scripture is often used to encourage people to share their faith and not to be ashamed. Paul, however, recognized that his gospel of peace was based on grace; a concept that the world had not yet known. The grace and faith message was so radical, so foreign to the people he was preaching to, that he had to say *"I am not ashamed."* Gal 1:6 *I marvel that you are turning away so soon from Him who called you in the **grace of Christ**, to a different gospel.* The people in Paul's day had a hard time receiving the grace of God because they had grown up under a performance based religious system not all that different than what's being preached in today's churches. Gal 1:7 *which is not another, but there are some who trouble you and want to pervert the gospel of Christ.* The gospel of Christ is perverted when you make grace void by attaching conditions, rules, or ordinances to it. For example, "you have to pray, fast, go to church, read your Bible, tithe, **and** believe in Jesus to be accepted in God's eyes." Paul goes on to say in Gal 1:8 *But even if we, or an angel from heaven, preach any other gospel to you than what we have preached to you, let him be accursed.* Paul felt so strongly about keeping the message of God's grace intact, that he basically repeated himself in verse 9 so that there would be no confusion.

I'm ready to settle this issue once and for all. Is the covenant that God has with the New Testament believer a conditional covenant? First let's look at the covenant God made with Noah after He flooded the earth. Gen 9:11 *Thus I established My covenant with you: Never again shall all flesh be cut off by the waters of the flood; never again shall there be a flood to destroy the earth.* Verse twelve goes on to say *This is the sign of the covenant which I make between Me and you, and every living creature that is with you, for perpetual generations.* It is important that we notice that God did not attach any conditions for man to keep with this covenant.

Now, let's look at the covenant God made with Abraham, which was conditional. In Genesis 17:4 God said *"**As for Me**, behold My covenant is with you and you shall be a father of many nations."* Gen 17:7 *And I will establish My covenant between Me and you and your descendents after you in their generation, for an everlasting covenant, to be God to you and your descendents after you.* God basically described how He would keep His end of the covenant, and goes on to describe the conditions Abraham and his descendants must keep. Gen 17:9 *And God said to Abraham; "**As for you**, you shall keep My covenant, you and your descendant after you."* In verse ten God says, *"This is My covenant which you shall keep…"* He then goes on to describe how they must be circumcised. We can see that the covenant with Noah was unconditional, but the covenant with Abraham had conditions.

When God gave the law to Moses, He basically expounded on the covenant. He further explained His side of the covenant or the blessings, and the peoples' side of the covenant, by the requirement of the law. God also lists the curses that would come upon the people if they did not keep all His commandments and statues. If you are not familiar with the old covenant blessings and curses, I would definitely recommend that you read Deuteronomy chapter 28. The curses listed in that chapter are absolutely horrible, and show God's awesome wrath against sin. You will have no choice but to thank God for placing all of that wrath on Jesus.

The people in the Old Testament were under a performance based system that instilled fear in the hearts of men. The modern day church has also adopted a performance based system with fear of rejection and the wrath of God as the main motivators. However, the prophet Isaiah has already, and in my estimation definitively solved the question of whether or not our new covenant is performance based. Isaiah 54:9-10 *For this* [the new covenant] *is like the **waters of Noah to me**; For as I have sworn that the waters of Noah would no longer cover the earth, so have I sworn that I would not be angry with you nor rebuke you, For the mountains shall depart and the hills be removed, but* *my kindness shall not depart from you, nor shall My* **covenant of peace** *be removed.* God says that the covenant of peace that we live under is the same type of covenant that He made with Noah – unconditional.

Despite this obvious truth, the most widely accepted doctrine is that we still have to earn the blessings of God through our obedience. The only way one could arrive at such a belief is to mix the old and new covenants. Jesus told us this would not work when He said you can't put new wine into old wineskins. I have recently heard many sermons on blocking the blessing. It seems like nine times out of ten the preacher starts with Joshua 1:8: *This Book of the Law shall not depart from your mouth, but you shall meditate in it day and night, that you may observe to do according to* **all** *that is written in it. For, then you will make your way prosperous, and then you will have good success.* The preacher will go on to say that the reason that the blessing of Abraham aren't showing up in your life is because they are being blocked by your disobedience. This type of preaching puts a religious yoke of bondage squarely on the shoulders of the congregation giving them an "I must do good to earn the blessing of God" mentality. This thinking is Old Testament and is actually anti-Christ in that it denies what Christ accomplished for us. Gal 3:13-14 *Christ has redeemed us from the curse of the law, having become a curse for us (for it is written, "Cursed is everyone who hangs on a tree") that the* **blessings** *of Abraham might come upon the Gentiles in Christ Jesus, that we might receive the promise of the Spirit* **through faith**. So then, do we receive the blessings of Abraham by works, or our obedience to a list of commandments, standards, and ordinances? The Bible makes it very clear that our faith in Jesus puts us into a position of right standing with God where we receive all of the blessings and none of the curses. Gal 3:26 *For you are all sons of God through faith in Christ Jesus.* Gal 3:29 *And if you are Christ's, then you are Abraham's seed, and heirs according to the promise.*

There may be some of you still having a hard time believing that God doesn't bless us proportionately to our performance. If that's you, listen to this: Eph 1:3 *Blessed be the God and Father of our Lord Jesus Christ, who* **has blessed us** *with every spiritual blessing in the heavenly places in Christ.* Notice that God has already blessed us with **every** spiritual blessing. This verse, and several verses like it, forever end the debate of whether or not we have to earn the blessings, or can block them through disobedience. It really doesn't matter what your personal opinion is because God has already blessed us with all spiritual blessings! Why would you try to obtain or earn something that you already have?

I have already established that God is a spirit and he deals with us in our new born again spirit. When the scripture says that we have been blessed with all spiritual blessings it is in fact talking about the spirit realm. The next logical question you should ask is what good does it do me to be blessed in the spirit realm, if I can't see it in the physical realm?

There are three key ingredients that we must understand to see the blessings we have in the spirit realm manifest in the physical realm. First, we cannot be conformed to the way this world thinks, but we must be transformed by renewing our minds to the truth that God has already blessed us. Secondly, as we have received salvation (by grace through faith) so shall we receive the blessings of God. In other words, we are saved, healed, prospered, and blessed by the grace of God, and not because we earned those things through obedience or any goodness on our part. The third ingredient is faith. We must put faith in the fact that God has already blessed us by His grace. Faith appropriates (brings to pass or manifests) what God has freely given to us by grace.

It is my observation that the people who have the hardest time receiving the blessings of God are the ones who've bought into the "sin blocks the blessing" mentality. *By the works of the law, no flesh shall be justified* (Gal 2:16). If you were to come to God and site your obedience to the law as your justification for receiving the blessing, you need to reread Gal 2:16. You must never get into a mindset that you **deserve** the blessings because you've earned them by doing good. James 2:10 *For whoever shall keep the whole law, and yet stumble in one point, he is guilty of all.* You should, on the other hand, thank God that He's not giving us what we deserve, but chose to bless us out of His goodness and grace. People, it's just this simple; you are either saved ([Greek word sozoed] made whole in every area of your life) by grace, or you are saved by works, but not a combination of the two (Rom 11:6). What does Hebrews 11:6 say? Does it say "without faith it is impossible to please God" or does it say "without obedience it is impossible to please God"? Obviously it says without faith. All disobedience is sin, and we know that Jesus paid the price for all sin, for all man, for all time. We know that we are blameless and above reproach in God's sight. We know that all blessings come from God. Therefore, if all blessings come from God, and He's not imputing our sins unto us, how can sin or disobedience block the blessing? Rom 8:32 *He who did not spare His own Son, but delivered Him up for us all, how shall He not with Him also **freely** give us all things?*

Chapter 7

The Definition of Stupidity

"The definition of stupidity is doing the same thing over and over and expecting different results." – Albert Einstein. The man makes a good point. We've also heard it said, "If it's not broke, don't fix it". Well, the religious system of our day is broke, and we do need to fix it. Also, it would be stupid to follow the same traditional belief systems that past generations have followed and expect to have a greater impact on our generation that they had on theirs. Many people view the church as irrelevant to their daily lives, and in effect, useless. I hate to say it, but the way many churches present salvation, and the Christian life, I'd have to agree.

I hope the previous chapter absolutely ruined your belief system. I hope it caused you to challenge and examine the sacred cows you may have been polishing in your life. We need to become like the people Paul ministered to in Acts 17 *in that they received the word with all readiness and searched the Scriptures daily to find out whether these things were so* (Acts 17:11). We too need to make the Bible our final authority, regardless of what our modern day religious Pharisees are preaching. Then they will say of us what they said of the early church; *"Those who have turned the world upside down have come here too"* (Act 17:6).

No one would argue that the New Testament church of Paul's day varies greatly from the average church in America. These people were not formally trained, nor did they have massive resources at their disposal. They did not have television or radio ministry, or even have access to a complete copy of the Bible. Despite all these things, they managed to spread the Gospel like wildfire to the ends of the known world. What was it about these people that caused them to sing praises to God when they were being burned at the stake or fed to lions? The answer is clear to me. These people had a better understanding of the true Gospel, a deeper revelation of the love of God, and a close intimate relationship with Him. Paul was preaching a pure undefiled gospel that he received straight from God. I'm sure most of us have played the telephone game as kids. Everybody sits in a circle, and someone starts a message by whispering it in the ear of the person next to them. Each person repeats the message to the person next to them until it reaches the original sender. It is always amazing to see how distorted the message can become even in a small circle. To a certain extent, this is what the church has done with the message of the gospel, and God's unconditional love and grace. It's a good thing we still have the accurate inspired Word of God neatly typed, bound, and covered in leather with the words of Christ in red. We need to follow God's example and exalt His word above all else. When we get back to the truth of the gospel, we will have the same and even better results than the New Testament church of Paul's day.

Most churches shun the message of God's unconditional love and grace, and favor a more condemning and belittling approach. They use fear as their main tool for motivating people to live a holy life, pay their tithes, and come to church. 1 John 4:18 *There is no fear in love: but perfect love casts out fear, because fear involves torment. But he who fears has not been made perfect in love.* Don't get me wrong. I'm all for preaching holiness after all, the word says, *"Be holy, for I am holy."* However, the church has been preaching holiness in a way that's opposite of what the scriptures teach us.

Holiness is the fruit not the root of salvation. 1 John 2:3 *Now by this we know that we know Him, if we keep His commandments.* This verse does not say if you want to know God, then keep His commandments. It says that once you truly know God, you will keep His commandments. Remember that religion will always have you focus on your outward actions and holiness. The preacher will tell you to do a, b, c, and d, and stop doing e, f, g, and h which amounts to nothing more than behavior modification. They are still trying to follow the Old Testament works system. If a man was caught committing adultery under the old covenant, he was to be stoned to death. Jesus said that under the new covenant, if a man looks at a woman to lust after her, he has already committed adultery in his heart. God wants our hearts, and is more concerned about the motives of our hearts than our outward physical actions. I'm sure the fear of death by stoning decreased the number of adulteries committed, but fear of punishment, not love for God was the motivating factor. 1 John 2:5 *But whoever keeps His word, truly the love of God is perfected in him. By this we know that we are in Him.* You can't give away what you don't have. We can't keep His commandments (to love the Lord your God with all your heart, soul, mind, and strength; and love your neighbor as yourself) if we haven't first received, and then been perfected by the love of God. Most people think God loves, or blesses, or is pleased with us in proportion to our performance. If you think this is true, then that's exactly how you will treat others. It is not until we understand that God's love and blessings are not tied to our performance that we can show God's type of agape (unconditional) love towards others as we are commanded.

People aren't beating down the church doors to get inside the way that they should be; therefore, we need a new approach. If you are a pastor of a church and you are forced to use fear, manipulation, or guilt to motivate the congregation to go out and witness to the lost, that should be a red flag. I once heard a pastor scream at the top of his lungs, "If your unsaved neighbors were to die and go to hell, their blood is on your foreheads. How can you sleep at night?" That would fall under the fear category. I've also heard: "How do you think God feels when you don't make time to read your Bible every day, or don't witness to your friends and invite them to church. How do you think that makes Him feel?" That would fall under the guilt category. So, the beat down church goes out, not motivated by love, and as Paul puts it "is like sounding brass or a clanging cymbal," and wonders why people don't respond. Here's what needs to happen. The pastor needs to take a couple of weeks off from flogging the people and telling them what miserable sinners they are, and preach about the unconditional love and grace of God. He needs to continue preaching on it until they get so full of the love of God, that it burns inside them like a fire that can't be held back. Then they will reach the point that Paul talks about where the love of Christ compels them.

All the good works that we do that are not motivated by love profits us nothing (1 Cor 13:3). 1 Corn 13:3 *each one's work will become clear; for the Day will declare it, because it will be revealed by fire; and the fire will test each one's work, of what sort it is.* The Bible is very clear that a Christian should do good works. We are to *be doers of the word and not hearers only deceiving ourselves* (James 1:22). However, this must come from the inside out and be motivated by love if we are to be rewarded for them. Titus 3:14 *And let our people also learn to maintain good works, to meet urgent needs, that they may not be unfruitful.*

Not only has the church been using fear to motivate its members to live holy, but it also uses fear as the main motive for salvation. We've all heard it, "turn or burn," "repent or else," "do you know how hot it is in hell?" You will, of course, get results from these tactics. You will literally scare the hell right out of people, but this is not the best method. Jude 1:16 shows us that some people do indeed need to be saved by fear. However, this is not the norm, and should be reserved for the "hard headed" individual. Romans 2:4 teaches us that it is the goodness of God that leads to repentance. We need to be preaching the Gospel of Peace. The way that the church is presenting salvation today, is one of the main reasons many people feel that the church is irrelevant to their daily lives. It is time for us to change our thinking. It is time for nothing short of a revolution to begin. Let us acknowledge every good thing that is in us in Christ Jesus. Let us return to the true Gospel which is the power of God unto salvation. Let us turn this world right side up to the praise and the glory of the most high God.

Chapter 8

<u>A Better Way</u>

Most people become a Christian so that they will not go to hell when they die. Although that is a good reason, missing hell should not be the goal of salvation. If the church presents the goal of salvation as having your sins forgiven and securing a place for yourself in heaven, then once you have responded to an altar call and received salvation, that's it. You've reached the goal! There's no point in going to church or reading your Bible. The Bible, however, teaches that the goal of salvation is a close intimate relationship with God through Jesus Christ. Let me explain. John 3:16 *For God so loved the world, that He gave His only begotten Son, that whoever believes in Him shall not perish, but have eternal life.* This is the way most people have interpreted this scripture: If you believe in Jesus, you will not go to hell, but live forever in heaven. That statement is true, but that is not what this scripture says. Everyone is going to live forever whether it's in heaven or hell. Let's go ahead and let Jesus define eternal life. John 17:*3 And this is eternal life, that they may know You, the only true God, and Jesus Christ whom You have sent.* Jesus defined eternal life as knowing God and knowing Him. The word "know" used there (ginosko in the Greek) goes beyond an intellectual level. It refers to an experiential, personal, and intimate understanding. The same word is used in Luke 1:34 when Mary said, *"How can this be, since I do not know a man?"* Therefore, Jesus defined eternal life as having a close, personal, and intimate relationship with God. Eternal life is a present tense reality for a believer, and not something that will take place in the sweet by and by. John 3:36 *He who believes in the Son **has** eternal life.* John 5:24 *Most assuredly I say to you, he who hears My word and believes in Him who sent me **has** eternal life.* With this in mind, let's reread John 3:16. *For God so loves the world, that He gave His only begotten Son, that whoever believes in Him shall not perish* [die spiritually since Jesus did that for us when He descended into hell, kicked the devil's butt, and gave us the keys to death, hell, and the grave] *but have* [present tense] *eternal life* [close, personal, intimate relationship with God]. We can see that the forgiveness of sins is not the point of salvation, but intimacy with God the Father is. Jesus dies to remove the barrier that stood between man and God – unforgiven sin. Therefore, anyone who views salvation as only forgiveness of sins, and stops there, is missing out on eternal life. For the most part, the church has been preaching the forgiveness of sins instead of relationship with God.

Jesus did not die for us out of pity for our impending doom. He died for us because of His love for us. He died to accomplish God's original plan for man. Rev 4:11 says that we were created for God's pleasure. God also created man to fellowship or commune with Him. Gen 3:8 shows that He used to walk and talk with Adam in the cool of the evening. Jesus came to restore that close intimate relationship between man and God.

The body of Christ needs to stop preaching a turn or burn salvation message, and start preaching the same Gospel that Paul preached. The church has boiled the gospel down to where it only deals with the eternal issues of heaven and hell. Most non-Christians are too busy dealing with their "hell on earth" that they don't care about their eternal future. People don't want to hear about how wonderful things are going to be if they go to heaven, when they're miserable, sick, broke, busted, and disgusted in the here and now. People don't need more religion, rules, commandments, or codes to adhere to. I believe people are looking for something real; something that will fill the emptiness inside. The only thing that will do that is intimate relationship (eternal life) with God the Father.

How do I know that the church is preaching a different gospel than the one Paul preached? I believe I can answer that question with a question. Has the "gospel" that's being preached at your church ever caused you to ask the question, "So what are you saying, are you saying we can just go live in sin?" Most likely it hasn't. Did you know that Paul had to answer this question four times in his gospel (the book of Romans)? "Can we just go live in sin?" is a very logical question when you hear about God's unconditional love and grace, the gift of salvation, and the gift of righteousness apart from works. The true gospel is nearly too good to be true news. The true gospel will set you free because it is the power of God unto salvation. Religious people hate seeing people set free. Paul, however, could not separate the grace of God from the gospel. Religious people will say "You can't tell people that they're free, then they'll just go live in sin. You've got to preach holiness." Titus 2:11-12 *For the grace of God that brings salvation has appeared to all men, teaching us that, denying ungodliness and worldly lust, we shall live soberly, righteously, and godly in the present age.* This passage of scripture tells that the grace of God teaches us to live holy. Verse 15 goes on to say, *Speak these things, exhort, and rebuke with all authority. Let no one despise you.* Religious and self righteous people will always despise the gospel of God's unconditional love and grace.

The Bible says draw near to God and He will draw near to you. God truly wants a relationship with you. Thanks to Jesus' atoning sacrifice, we are able to enter into the holy of holies and commune with God. Thanks to the new covenant, God is no longer in an adversarial position towards mankind. He is our loving Father. Through faith in Jesus, we are His sons and daughters, and are accepted in the Beloved. It has been my experience that the more you understand the loving character and nature of God, the more you want to worship Him by serving and obeying Him. God never desired burnt offerings and sacrifices, or obedience through fear. Nor did He desire obedience as a motive for earning blessings. God wants your heart. He knows that once He gets your heart, He'll get your service.

Everyone has a call of God on their life. However, not everyone responds to God's call. Eph 2:10 *For we are His workmanship created in Christ Jesus for good works, which God prepared beforehand that we should walk in them.* The more you build your relationship with God, the more you will soften your heart towards the things of God. You will then be able to recognize the gifts that He has given you; *For the equipping of the saints for the work of ministry for the edifying of the body of Christ.* We are all members of the body of Christ and are called to do our share so that the body can grow. The point I'm trying to make, is that although there's work to be done, we must keep our relationship with God our number one priority. We must be careful not to fall into the religious mind set that God's love and acceptance of us is based on our good works.

Finally, we need to recognize and preach everything that Jesus purchased for us at Calvary. In John 10:10 Jesus said, *"I have come that you may have life, and have it more abundantly."* If a lost person were to listen to a Christian radio station for one day, they would have to assume that the Christian life was no better than theirs. They'll hear songs of: desperation, wailing and travailing, songs questioning whether or not He's even there, or if He hears our prayers. Worst of all, they'd hear songs about how we're still going to praise the Lord despite all the tragedy and hardship He causes in our lives. It is very rare to hear a song praising God for this life of victory that He's given us. In fact if you do hear one, you'd better turn it up because chances are the next song will be begging God to help us barely get by until the trumpet blows. Wake up church! Has He not *given us all things that pertain to life and godliness* (2 Peter 1:3)? This life is not going to be all peaches and cream. We will have problems that come our way. John 16:33b *In this world you will have tribulation; but be of good cheer, I have overcome the world.* Not only did Jesus overcome the world, but He gave us the victory that overcomes the world – our faith (1 John 5:4).

Therefore, let us focus on the abundant God-kind of life that Jesus died to give us. Jesus has surely *borne our sicknesses and carried our sorrows* (Isaiah 53:4). *He was wounded for our transgressions, He was bruised for our iniquities; The chastisement for our peace was upon Him, and by His stripes we are healed* (Isaiah 53:5). Jesus was forsaken by God on the cross so that you and I would never be forsaken by God. Jesus redeemed us from the curse of the law (see Deuteronomy 28:45-68). We no longer have to live a miserable defeated life of sickness, poverty, and depression. *The Lord takes pleasure in the prosperity of His servants* (Ps 35:27) and *it is His good pleasure to give us the kingdom* (Luke 12:32). It is way beyond the scope and purpose of this book to fully teach on healing, faith, biblical prosperity, prayer, or gifts of the Spirit. My goal was to open the eyes of the church by exposing the religious traditions of man that make the word of God of no effect. With that in mind, examine the fruit in your church, and the fruit in your own life. Are peoples' lives being radically transformed? Is the gospel of the kingdom spreading like wild fire? Is the fact that you're a Christian obvious to the people you come in contact with every day? Could you say the church, as a whole, is operating in the power of the Holy Spirit in like manner as the church in the Book of Acts? If not, we need a change. I pray that the eyes of your understanding have been enlightened to the point that you can no longer claim ignorance. I pray that His Word will burn in your heart until you are compelled by the love of God together with the power of the Holy Spirit to rise up and take action.

Chapter 9

<u>Free at Last</u>

If you abide in My word, you are My disciples indeed. And you shall know the truth, and the truth shall make you free (John 8:31-32). John 8:36 *Therefore if the Son makes you free, you shall be free indeed.* We have been set free from sin and the bondage it had over us. I believe I have already made my next point, but I want to make it again so that no one misunderstands the grace of God. Gal 5:13 *For you brethren, have been called to liberty; only do not use liberty as an opportunity for the flesh, but through love serve one another.* The grace of God does not make you free to sin, but it makes you free from sin. Anyone that hears this message and says, "Alright, since God's love for me is unconditional, now I can go live in sin," they need to flip to the back of this book and get born- again. 1 John 3:3 *And everyone who has this hope in Him purifies himself, just as He is pure.*

The spirit of Christ living inside you will cause you to want to live holy. Every time you sin, you are yielding yourself to your enemy. *For he that sows to his flesh will of the flesh reap corruption* (Gal 6:8). Although sin doesn't affect your born-again spirit that has been sealed, it will corrupt your body. For me, it all boils down to this, you will truly be happier living a holier life, than a life that you are constantly yielding to sin. We must not believe the lie of the devil that sin is more fun than obedience, or that his system of the world is better than God's system which is the Kingdom. Rom 8:5 *For to be carnally* [ruled by your emotions or five senses] *minded is death, but to be spiritually* [ruled by the Word of God] *minded is life and peace.* That's not a very tough decision. Let's choose life and peace.

If you have received the truths I have presented in this book, then you have been set free from certain religious traditions of man. I must now caution you not to be like the person described in Matt 13:20-21. *But he who received the seed on stony places, this is he who hears the word and immediately receives it with joy; yet he has no root in himself, but endures only for a while. For when tribulation or persecution arises because of the word, immediately he stumbles.* You will suffer persecution when you try to share these truths with religious people. Some of the things presented in this book are radically different than what's been widely taught and accepted in the church today. People seem to have a resistance to change. Challenging a person's beliefs causes them to do something very painful – think for themselves. It is important to search the scriptures for yourself and meditate on the biblical principals presented in this book. We are told in Romans 12:2 not to be conformed to the world, but to be transformed by the renewing of our minds.

I believe the truths presented in this book are so important, so life changing, that I rejoice when I am persecuted for sharing them. The apostles had the same attitude in Acts 5:41. *So they departed from the presence of the council, rejoicing that they were counted worthy to suffer shame for His name.* I've heard it said, "If you never run into the devil, it's because you're both going in the same direction."

Have you been set free? *Stand fast therefore in the liberty by which Christ has made us free, and do not be entangled again with a yoke of bondage* (Gal 5:1).

The words "stand fast" imply action on our part. In Gal 2:4 Paul wrote to the believers of his day warning them saying *"false brethren [were] secretly brought in who came in by stealth to spy out our liberty which we have in Christ Jesus, that they might bring us into bondage."* Notice that the attack on the freedom we have in Christ Jesus comes from the church and not the world. So how do we stand fast? First of all, we can't keep sitting under false doctrine and wrong teaching. The same way that faith comes by hearing, so does fear, doubt, and unbelief. You can not constantly listen to preaching full of religious traditions that are contrary to the word of God with out it creeping into your mind and affecting your heart. This is why we are told to guard our hearts with all diligence. There are plenty of churches out there that are doing more harm than good. You need to find a Bible believing, and therefore Spirit filled church that's bearing fruit. Go to a place where lives are being transformed, people are being healed, saved, delivered, prospered, filled with the Spirit, and where the word of faith and a victorious Christian life are being preached. If you don't know of such a place, just ask God. Acknowledge Him in all your ways, and He shall direct your path. Remember that God's church is the people and not the building. You could always find a group of like minded believers, and come together for church in someone's living room. This was the case for the believers of Paul's day. This is also happening in countries where Christians are being persecuted. It's far too easy to blend in at a large seeker-friendly church and never get involved. We've all been given gifts, let us use them! (Rom 12:6)

"Oh God, send revival! Pour out your Spirit we're hungry!" How many times have you heard that in church? I once saw an eight foot banner that said "We're praying for revival". Some of you are probably thinking "What's wrong with that? I helped make that banner." First of all, God's already poured out His Spirit in Acts chapter two. Acts 2:4 *and they were all filled with the Holy Spirit and began to speak with other tongues, as the Spirit gave them utterance.* Some of the people that heard this were amazed, but others mocked them supposing they were drunk. Peter stood up and explained in Acts 2:16 *But **this** is what was spoken by the prophet Joel;* Acts 2:17 *And it shall come to pass in the last days, says God, that I will pour out My Spirit on* *all flesh.* Also, when we get the whole church together to pray for God to send revival we are basically insinuating that for some reason God is holding back revival. Perhaps if we get enough people to beg, plead, wail and travail loud enough, we can storm the gates of heaven until God has no choice but to send revival. Can you not see what's wrong with this mindset? God is on our side. Don't you think God wants the lifeless segments of His body (the church) revived more than we do? We're not waiting on God to move, He's waiting on us to move. He has literally given us all things that pertain to life and godliness. Still, people have the audacity to cry out, "Oh God give us more, we need more of you." The same power that raised Jesus from the dead; the most powerful force ever displayed on this earth is alive and well in every Spirit filled believer. Yet people beg God to move on their behalf. *God is well able to do exceeding, abundantly above all that we can ask or think, according to the power that works in us* (Eph 3:20). I hope people can use this book as some sort of catalyst or spark to ignite the powder keg that has been lying dormant inside of them.

Do you want to start a revival in your church? The first thing you need to do is to be endued with the power from on high, by receiving the baptism of the Holy Spirit. Then you have to shake off the chains of religious bondage. It would then be necessary to get a revelation of how much God loves you and that His love, favor, or blessings are not based on your performance. You should then learn the laws that govern faith, and begin to recognize and walk in the authority you've been given. Go out motivated by love, empowered by the Holy Spirit and heal the sick, raise the dead, open a few blind eyes and deaf ears, and you will have all the revival you can handle. You'll have to make a new banner that reads, "Standing room only". In other words, let's be the church that God has called us to be. Whether you like it or not, Jesus has passed us the torch. We have all the answers to life's questions. The church is God's chosen vessel to bring His message of love and grace to the world. If the church would start doing what we were told to do, people would be beating the doors down to try and get what we've got. We need to stop **having** church twice a week and start **being** the church.

Finally my brethren, stir yourselves up! When people hear the word "Christian" they should automatically associate it with a life of world-overcoming power and victory. Acknowledge every good thing that is in you in Christ Jesus. You have been predestined to be conformed to the image of His Son (Rom 8:29). *Moreover, whom He predestined these He also called; whom He called these He also justified; and whom He justified, these He also glorified* (Rom 8:30). The Bible says that Jesus was the firstborn among many brethren (Rom 8:29). Therefore, we are heirs of God and joint-heirs with Christ (Rom 8:17). John 14:12 *Most assuredly, I say to you, he who believes in Me, the works that I do he will do also; and greater works than these he will do, because I go to My Father.* Won't someone rise up? Won't someone pick up the torch that Jesus left for us and run with it? The eyes of the Lord run to and fro throughout the whole earth to show Himself strong on behalf of those who love Him. We are the light of the world. We are the salt of the earth. We've each been given a race to run. Therefore, run in such a way as to win. Before I finish this book, I must exhort you one more time to stand fast in the liberty by which

Christ has made you free, and do not be entangled again with a religious yoke of bondage. I leave you with one last passage of scripture:

"For I am persuaded that neither death nor life, nor angels nor principalities nor powers, nor things present nor things to come, nor height nor depth, not any other created thing, shall be able to separate us from the love of God which is in Christ Jesus our Lord. (Rom 8:38-39)

A Prayer to Receive Salvation

My friends, you have heard the true gospel by reading this book. Choosing to receive Jesus as Your Lord and Savior is the most important decision you'll ever make! God's Word promises, *"That if you confess with your mouth the Lord Jesus and believe in your heart that God has raised Him from the dead, you will be saved. For with the heart one believes unto righteousness, and with the mouth confession is made unto salvation"* (Romans 10:9-10). *"For whoever calls on the name of the Lord shall be saved"* (Romans 10:13).

By His grace, God has already done everything to provide salvation. Your part is to simply believe and receive. Pray this out loud: "Jesus I confess that you are my Lord and Savior. I believe in my heart that God raised You from the dead. By faith in Your Word, I receive salvation now. Thank you for saving me!"

The very moment you commit your life to Jesus Christ, the truth of His Word instantly comes to pass in your spirit. Now that you're born again, you are a brand new creation!

Receiving the Holy Spirit

Most of the people that I know who've received the baptism of the Holy Spirit, received it while a spirit filled believer laid hands on them. However it doesn't have to come that way. As His child, your loving heavenly Father wants to give you the supernatural power you need to live this new live. *For everyone who asks receives, and he who seeks finds, and to him who knocks it will be opened... how much more will your heavenly Father give the Holy Spirit to those who ask Him?*

All you have to do is ask, believe, and receive. Pray this: "Father, I recognize my need for Your power to live this new life. Please fill me with Your Holy Spirit. By faith, I receive it right now! Thank you for baptizing me! Holy Spirit, you are welcome in my life!"

Congratulations! Now you're filled with God's supernatural power! Some syllables from a language you don't recognize will rise up from your heart to your mouth, (1 Cor 14:14). As you speak them out loud by faith, you're releasing God's power from within and building yourself up in the spirit (1 Cor 14:4). You can do this whenever you like!